E
551.57
SCHUH

### Earth in Action

# Avalanches

by Mari Schuh

**Consulting Editor:** Gail Saunders-Smith, PhD

**Consultant:** Susan L. Cutter, PhD
Carolina Distinguished Professor and Director,
Hazards & Vulnerability Research Institute
Department of Geography, University of South Carolina

Mankato, Minnesota

Pebble Plus is published by Capstone Press,
151 Good Counsel Drive, P.O. Box 669, Mankato, Minnesota 56002.
www.capstonepress.com

Copyright © 2010 by Capstone Press, a Capstone Publishers company. All rights reserved.
No part of this publication may be reproduced in whole or in part, or stored in a retrieval system, or transmitted in any
form or by any means, electronic, mechanical, photocopying, recording, or otherwise, without written permission of the
publisher. For information regarding permission, write to Capstone Press,
151 Good Counsel Drive, P.O. Box 669, Dept. R, Mankato, Minnesota 56002.
Printed in the United States of America, North Mankato, Minnesota.

 Books published by Capstone Press are manufactured with paper
containing at least 10 percent post-consumer waste.

*Library of Congress Cataloging-in-Publication Data*
Schuh, Mari, 1975–
　　Avalanches / by Mari Schuh.
　　p. cm. — (Pebble Plus. Earth in action)
　　Includes bibliographical references and index.
　　ISBN 978-1-4296-3437-3 (lib. bdg.)
　　1. Avalanches — Juvenile literature.　I. Title.　II. Series.
QC929.A8S348 2010
551.57'848 — dc22　　　　　　　　　　　　　　　　　　　　　　　2009002163

Summary: Describes avalanches, how they occur, and the damage they cause.

**Editorial Credits**
Erika L. Shores, editor; Lori Bye, designer; Wanda Winch, media researcher

**Photo Credits**
Art Life Images, Inc./age fotostock/nevio doz, 21; iTravelstock Collection/Bill Stevenson, 17
Getty Images Inc./AFP/Jose Navarro, 13; Aurora/Scott Warren, cover
iStockphoto/jkey, 7
Peter Arnold/Biosphoto/BIOS-Auteurs (droits geres)/Denis Bringard, 9
Shutterstock/auddmin, 11; Fredrik Johansson, 15; Kapu, 1; Mikhail Pogosov, 5
USGS Glacier Field Station, Northern Rocky Mountain Science Center/Mark Dundas, 19

**The author dedicates this book to ardent supporter Gene Mayer of Kenosha, Wisconsin.**

## Note to Parents and Teachers

The Earth in Action set supports national science standards related to earth science.
This book describes and illustrates avalanches. The images support early readers in
understanding the text. The repetition of words and phrases helps early readers learn new
words. This book also introduces early readers to subject-specific vocabulary words, which are
defined in the Glossary section. Early readers may need assistance to read some words and to
use the Table of Contents, Glossary, Read More, Internet Sites, and Index sections of the book.

032010
5699R

# Table of Contents

What Is an Avalanche? . . . . . . . 4
What Causes Avalanches? . . . . . 8
During an Avalanche . . . . . . . . 10
Staying Safe . . . . . . . . . . . . . . 14
After an Avalanche . . . . . . . . . 18

Glossary . . . . . . . . . . . . . . . . . 22
Read More . . . . . . . . . . . . . . . 23
Internet Sites . . . . . . . . . . . . . . 23
Index . . . . . . . . . . . . . . . . . . . 24

# What Is an Avalanche?

An avalanche is

a huge amount of snow

sliding down a mountain.

The Alps in Europe

have the most avalanches.

Many other avalanches

happen in the Rocky Mountains

in the United States.

Alps

# What Causes Avalanches?

Unstable snow causes avalanches.

Earthquakes, warm weather,

and wind cause snow to shift.

Skiers and loud noises

also set off avalanches.

# During an Avalanche

A huge pile of snow breaks

loose during an avalanche.

The snow speeds down

the mountain with great power.

Ice, rocks, and trees can slide down, too. An avalanche buries everything in its path.

# Staying Safe

Signs warn people of danger.

Green signs mean avalanches are very unlikely.

Red signs mean an avalanche could happen.

Experts cause small avalanches far away from people.

These small avalanches prevent bigger ones later.

# After an Avalanche

Scientists measure damage from an avalanche using the destructive force scale. This scale is based on how much snow is in the avalanche.

Rescue teams work hard to find avalanche survivors. They dig out people buried in the snow.

# Glossary

**Alps** — a large mountain range in Europe

**avalanche** — a mass of snow, rocks, ice, or soil that slides down a mountain slope; avalanches are also called snow slides.

**danger** — a situation that is not safe

**destructive force scale** — a scale that measures the damage from an avalanche from one to five, with five being the highest.

**earthquake** — the sudden shaking of the earth's surface

**prevent** — to keep from happening

**survivor** — someone who lives through a disaster or horrible event

**unstable** — not steady or firm; unstable snow might move or fall.

# Read More

**Bishop, Amanda.** *Avalanche and Landslide Alert!* Disaster Alert! New York: Crabtree Publishing, 2005.

**Bullard, Lisa.** *Avalanches.* Pull Ahead Books: Forces of Nature. Minneapolis: Lerner, 2008.

**Hamilton, John.** *Avalanches.* Nature's Fury. Edina, Minn.: Abdo, 2006.

# Internet Sites

FactHound offers a safe, fun way to find Internet sites related to this book. All of the sites on FactHound have been researched by our staff.

Here's all you do:
Visit *www.facthound.com*

FactHound will fetch the best sites for you!

# Index

Alps, 6
damage, 18
danger, 14
destructive force scale, 18
earthquakes, 8
experts, 16
ice, 12
mountains, 4, 6, 10
noises, 8

rescue teams, 20
rocks, 12
Rocky Mountains, 6
scientists, 18
signs, 14
skiers, 8
survivors, 20
trees, 12
weather, 8
wind, 8

Word Count: 160
Grade: 1
Early-Intervention Level: 24